TRIUMPH
over
TRAUMA

A Self-Paced, Guided Workbook to Help You Work through Your Past Trauma

Jendayi A. Stafford

Coloring pages by Heather Sydnor

ISBN 978-1-0980-0930-4 (paperback)
ISBN 978-1-0980-1833-7 (hardcover)
ISBN 978-1-0980-0931-1 (digital)

Christian Faith Publishing, Inc.
832 Park Avenue
Meadville, PA 16335
www.christianfaithpublishing.com

Printed in the United States of America

To you and your journey of healing!

Healing is a process, not a race. It is not equal in time, or in appearance.

A traumatic event in life is like a scratch on a record. Every time the record player,
or your mind, runs over the scratch, it skips. This skipping record thought pattern
is called rumination. Until we're able to fill the scratch, it will keep skipping.
—*Two Guys on Your Head*: Grief

You don't have to ever verbally tell your story, but it writing it down is therapeutic to you in mind
body and soul.

There is no greater agony than bearing an untold story inside you.
—Maya Angelou

CONTENTS

INTRODUCTION

Over the past several years, I have worked with many people who, like yourself, have been affected by trauma. Through different variations of trials, I was able to help many individuals find ways that worked for them to be able to overcome the negative effects of their trauma.

I too have personally dealt with trauma, and I am aware of the effects that it can have on a person. I have suffered from panic attacks, flashbacks, nightmares, and feelings of being overwhelmed. I know what it feels like to be in a store and have to run out because I suddenly begin to cry hysterically because I feel trapped and like I cannot breathe. I have had flashbacks buckle my knees, and I start to panic as people gather around me to see if I'm all right, causing me to hyperventilate.

This journal was written as a result of a tool that I have used personally and professionally to help people overcome their traumatic event. With the use of different therapeutic techniques, such as narrative therapy and mindfulness, you are able to retell and rewrite your story and relinquish the power it has over you. This is not a "cure all," but this is a tool that can be used as a first step to helping you overcome your trauma and regaining your power!

How to Best Use This Workbook

You may have dealt with many different traumatic events in your lifetime, but I want you to use this journal to focus on just one of them. You may not feel as though all sections apply to you and the traumatic event that you experienced. That is okay. I still encourage you to fill them out to the best of your ability.

Helpful Resources Available if You or Family/Friends Are in Need of Mental Health Support

YOU matter! *** **YOU** are loved! *** **YOU** are amazing! *** **YOU** are more than a conqueror! *** **YOU** have greatness inside of **YOU**! *** **YOU** are beautiful! *** **YOU ARE NOT** the lies that people said/say about **YOU**! *** **YOU** are not what has happened / is happening to **YOU**! *** **YOU** are unstoppable! *** **YOU** were created for a specific purpose that only **YOU** can fulfill!

As you begin to work through this workbook, there may be some strong emotions that are brought to the surface. If you are finding yourself in a "not so good place" mentally, then please call someone! Write down at least three people that you trust and can call and talk to.

1. Name: _____ Number: _____
2. Name: _____ Number: _____
3. Name: _____ Number: _____

If you do not have anyone whom you can reach out to, then please call the **National Suicide Prevention Lifeline: 800-273-TALK [8255]**. The **National Suicide Prevention Lifeline: 800-273-TALK [8255]** provides FREE 24-7 support that is confidential! You can find more information on their website: SuicidePreventionLifeline.org.

Other Resources

1. **notOK**

   When you can't think of the right words, the notOK App™ takes the guesswork out of getting the help and support you need through immediate support from your friends, family, or peer network.

   Simply open the app, tap the notOK™ button, and a text message along with your current GPS location will be sent to your pre-selected contacts. (https://www.notokapp.com/)

2. **CircleOf6**

   It's fast, easy-to-use and private. Originally designed for college students to prevent sexual violence, we also know it's handy for teenagers, parents, friends, or all communities seeking to foster healthy relationships and safety.

   Need help getting home? Need an interruption? Two taps will let your circle know where you are and how they can help. Circle of 6 app for iPhone and Android makes it quick and easy to reach the 6 people you choose.

   It's the mobile way to look out for each other on campus or when you're out for the night. A simple tool to prevent violence before it happens. (https://www.notokapp.com/).

3. **R3** stands for "Recognize, Respond, and Refer." It is a self-evaluation of whether or not you or someone you know is in an abusive relationship.

    R3 is based on the HITS screening tool, a four-item questionnaire which stands for Hurt, Insult, Threaten, and Scream and was created to give physicians an easy-to-use tool to assess for intimate partner violence.

    The R3 app can be used by anyone to help identify if someone is experiencing abuse. The app also has specific information and resources for health care professionals. (https://www.techsafety.org/r3app/)

4. **The Crisis Text Line** is a free and anonymous 24-7 service for those who are experiencing a mental health crisis. The Crisis Text Line connects you to a trained mental health professional immediately. All you have to do is text the word *HOME* to 741741 and you will receive a text from one of the trained mental health counselors. Their website is CrisisTextLine.org.

5. **Therapist Finder** is an app that can be downloaded on your phone in order to help you locate a therapist in your area. Therapist Finder shows a list of professionals in your area, including psychologists, mental health counselors, marriage and family therapists, as well as life coaches.

MY STORY

In this section, I want you to write your story. This story is of the traumatic event which you are wanting to focus on. I want you to be as descriptive as you want; but the more descriptive you are now, the more helpful it will be later on throughout the journal. Remember, you are not currently in the situation which you are about to write about!

This is MY story:
(use additional paper if needed)

_____
_____
_____
_____
_____
_____
_____
_____
_____
_____
_____
_____
_____
_____
_____
_____
_____
_____
_____
_____
_____
_____
_____

What is the one element of this story that you would change?
(Just focus on one element within your story.)

_____
_____
_____
_____
_____
_____
_____
_____
_____

In regard to the one element that you would change, what would you replace it with?
(This may take much thought, so take your time. It doesn't have to be perfect.)

_____
_____
_____
_____
_____
_____
_____
_____
_____

Why would you replace that one element with whatever you wrote about on the previous page?

_____
_____
_____
_____
_____
_____
_____
_____

What lessons, if any, did you learn from your experience?

_____
_____
_____
_____
_____
_____

MY FREE SPACE

```
┌ ─ ─ ─ ─ ─ ─ ─ ─ ─ ─ ─ ┐
│                       │
│                       │
│     <<insert image>>  │
│                       │
│                       │
└ ─ ─ ─ ─ ─ ─ ─ ─ ─ ─ ─ ┘
```

This section is for you to be able to use however you see fit. Referring back to **My Story** and **Word Association**, I want you to use this space freely to get your own thoughts out. Draw, scribble, write a poem! However you see fit to express the emotions, thoughts, and feelings toward the event you described, do it! This section is the least scripted within this journal. You are unlimited and free to use these next few pages in whatever way you see fit!

JENDAYI A. STAFFORD

SENSORY AND IMAGERY

<<insert image>>

These next few sections focus on sensory and imagery. You are going to mentally revisit the traumatic event, focusing on very specific sensory areas (**sight, sound, smell, taste, and touch/feel**). Remember, you are no longer in that situation! This is a big part of the healing process and should not be rushed. If you begin to feel overwhelmed during any part of this journaling activity, then step away from it for a little bit. Regroup yourself and come back to it when you are ready.

There is no timeline on the healing process! If you need to step away for a moment's time, please do so, but please come back to it. Romans 8:37 says that we are more than a conqueror! Gather your thoughts and come back ready to conquer!

WHAT DID YOU SEE?

For this section, I want you to focus solely on what you **saw** in association with your traumatic event. There is space for you to write your response, and/or draw your response to the following questions. What can you remember **seeing** right before you experienced your trauma? (Try to think about the first thirty minutes or less leading up to your traumatic experience. Be very specific and detailed, and remember that you are not currently in that situation!)

_____
_____
_____
_____
_____
_____
_____
_____
_____
_____
_____
_____
_____
_____
_____
_____
_____
_____
_____
_____
_____
_____
_____
_____
_____

If you would like to, use this space to draw what you **saw** right before the trauma. What do you remember **seeing** during the time that your traumatic event was taking place? (Focus on what you **saw** while the trauma was taking place. Again, be specific and detailed. Remember that you are not currently in that situation!)

If you would like to, use this space to draw what you **saw** during the traumatic event. What can you remember **seeing** immediately after you experienced the traumatic event? (Try to think about the thirty minutes or so that followed your traumatic experience. Be very specific and detailed, and remember that you are not currently in that situation!)

If you would like to, use this space to draw what you **saw** following the traumatic event.

WHAT DID YOU HEAR?

```
┌ ─ ─ ─ ─ ─ ─ ─ ─ ─ ─ ─ ┐

│                       │

│                       │

│     <<insert image>>  │

│                       │

│                       │

└ ─ ─ ─ ─ ─ ─ ─ ─ ─ ─ ─ ┘
```

For this section, I want you to focus solely on what you **heard** in association with your traumatic event. There is space for you to write your response, and/or draw your response to the following questions. What can you remember **hearing** right before you experienced your trauma? (Try to think about the first thirty minutes or less leading up to your traumatic experience. Be very specific and detailed and remember that you are not currently in that situation!)

_____

_____

_____

_____

_____

_____

_____

_____

_____

_____

_____

_____

_____

_____

If you would like to, use this space to draw what you **heard** before the traumatic event. What do you remember **hearing** during the time that your traumatic event was taking place? (Focus on what you **heard** while the trauma was taking place. Again, be specific and detailed. Remember that you are not currently in that situation!)

If you would like to, use this space to draw what you **heard** during the traumatic event. What can you remember **hearing** immediately after you experienced the traumatic event? (Try to think about the thirty minutes or so that followed your traumatic experience. Be very specific and detailed, and remember that you are not currently in that situation!)

If you would like to, use this space to draw what you **heard** after the traumatic event.

WHAT DID YOU SMELL?

For this section, I want you to focus solely on what you **smelled** in association with your traumatic event. There is space for you to write your response, and/or draw your response to the following questions. What can you remember **smelling** right before you experienced your trauma? (Try to think about the first thirty minutes or less leading up to your traumatic experience. Be very specific and detailed, and remember that you are not currently in that situation!)

_____

_____

_____

_____

_____

_____

_____

_____

_____

_____

_____

_____

_____

_____

_____

_____

_____

_____

If you would like to, use this space to draw what you **smelled** before the traumatic event.

What do you remember **smelling** during the time that your traumatic event was taking place? (Focus on what you **smelled** while the trauma was taking place. Again, be specific and detailed. Remember that you are not currently in that situation!)

_____
_____
_____
_____
_____
_____
_____
_____
_____
_____
_____
_____
_____
_____
_____
_____
_____
_____
_____

If you would like to, use this space to draw what you **smelled** during the traumatic event.

What can you remember **smelling** immediately after you experienced the traumatic event? (Try to think about the thirty minutes or so that followed your traumatic experience. Be very specific and detailed, and remember that you are not currently in that situation!)

_____
_____
_____
_____
_____
_____
_____
_____
_____
_____
_____
_____
_____
_____
_____
_____
_____
_____

If you would like to, use this space to draw what you **smelled** after the traumatic event.

WHAT DID YOU TASTE?

```
┌ ─ ─ ─ ─ ─ ─ ─ ─ ─ ─ ┐
│                     │
│                     │
│    <<insert image>> │
│                     │
│                     │
└ ─ ─ ─ ─ ─ ─ ─ ─ ─ ─ ┘
```

For this section, I want you to focus solely on what you **tasted** in association with your traumatic event. There is space for you to write your response, and/or draw your response to the following questions. What can you remember **tasting** right before you experienced your trauma? (Try to think about the first thirty minutes or less leading up to your traumatic experience. Be very specific and detailed, and remember that you are not currently in that situation!)

_____

_____

_____

_____

_____

_____

_____

_____

_____

_____

_____

_____

_____

_____

_____

_____

_____

If you would like to, use this space to draw what you **tasted** before the traumatic event.

What do you remember **tasting** during the time that your traumatic event was taking place? (Focus on what you **tasted** while the trauma was taking place. Again, be specific and detailed. Remember that you are not currently in that situation!)

_____

_____

_____

_____

_____

_____

_____

_____

_____

_____

_____

_____

_____

_____

_____

_____

_____

_____

_____

If you would like to, use this space to draw what you **tasted** during the traumatic event.

What can you remember **tasting** immediately after you experienced the traumatic event? (Try to think about the thirty minutes or so that followed your traumatic experience. Be very specific and detailed, and remember that you are not currently in that situation!)

_____
_____
_____
_____
_____
_____
_____
_____
_____
_____
_____
_____
_____
_____
_____
_____
_____
_____
_____

If you would like to, use this space to draw what you **tasted** after the traumatic event.

WHAT DID YOU FEEL (PHYSICALLY)?

<<insert image>>

For this section, I want you to focus solely on what you **physically felt** in association with your traumatic event. There is space for you to write your response, and/or draw your response to the following questions. What can you remember **physically feeling** right before you experienced your trauma? (Try to think about the first thirty minutes or less leading up to your traumatic experience. Be very specific and detailed, and remember that you are not currently in that situation!)

_____
_____
_____
_____
_____
_____
_____
_____
_____
_____
_____
_____
_____
_____
_____
_____
_____
_____

If you would like to, use this space to draw what you **physically felt** before the traumatic event.

What do you remember **physically feeling** during the time that your traumatic event was taking place? (Focus on what you **physically felt** while the trauma was taking place. Again, be specific and detailed. Remember that you are not currently in that situation!)

_____
_____
_____
_____
_____
_____
_____
_____
_____
_____
_____
_____
_____
_____
_____
_____
_____
_____

If you would like to, use this space to draw what you **physically felt** during the traumatic event.

What can you remember **physically feeling** immediately after you experienced the traumatic event? (Try to think about the thirty minutes or so that followed your traumatic experience. Be very specific and detailed, and remember that you are not currently in that situation!)

_____
_____
_____
_____
_____
_____
_____
_____
_____
_____
_____
_____
_____
_____
_____
_____
_____

If you would like to, use this space to draw what you **physically felt** after the traumatic event.

WHAT DID YOU FEEL (EMOTIONALLY)?

<<insert image>>

For this section, I want you to focus solely on what you **emotionally felt** in association with your traumatic event. There is space for you to write your response, and/or draw your response to the following questions. What can you remember **emotionally feeling** right before you experienced your trauma? (Try to think about the first thirty minutes or less leading up to your traumatic experience. Be very specific and detailed, and remember that you are not currently in that situation!)

_____
_____
_____
_____
_____
_____
_____
_____
_____
_____
_____
_____
_____
_____
_____
_____
_____

If you would like to, use this space to draw what you **emotionally felt** before the traumatic event.

What do you remember **emotionally feeling** during the time that your traumatic event was taking place? (Focus on what you **emotionally felt** while the trauma was taking place. Again, be specific and detailed. Remember that you are not currently in that situation!)

_____
_____
_____
_____
_____
_____
_____
_____
_____
_____
_____
_____
_____
_____
_____
_____
_____

If you would like to, use this space to draw what you **emotionally felt** during the traumatic event.

What can you remember **emotionally feeling** immediately after you experienced the traumatic event? (Try to think about the thirty minutes or so that followed your traumatic experience. Be very specific and detailed, and remember that you are not currently in that situation!)

_____
_____
_____
_____
_____
_____
_____
_____
_____
_____
_____
_____
_____
_____
_____
_____
_____
_____

If you would like to, use this space to draw what you **emotionally felt** after the traumatic event.

THIS IS MY STORY

Build on your original story by incorporating the **sights**, **sounds**, **smells**, **tastes**, **physical feelings**, and **emotional feelings** that you have just focused on. Rewrite your story as you remember it, including any additional information that you recall **seeing**, **hearing**, **smelling**, **tasting**, **physically** and **emotionally feeling** before, during, and after the traumatic event. Again, remember that you are not currently in that situation! (Use additional paper if needed.)

_____
_____
_____
_____
_____
_____
_____
_____
_____
_____
_____
_____
_____
_____
_____
_____
_____
_____
_____
_____
_____
_____
_____
_____
_____
_____

WORD ASSOCIATION

<<insert image>>

Proverbs 18:21 (NKJV) says,

> Death and life are in the power of the tongue,
> And those who love it will eat its fruit.

You need to start learning how to speak life into your situations and over yourself! Don't let those negative things that people say about you manifest themselves. You have the power to counter-act those death-filled words and phrases and speak life against them! You are not the trauma that you have experienced! Rather, you are a conqueror of the very event that has tried to break you!

Provided is a list of words that can be used for the exercise below. Do not feel obligated to have to use one of the words on the list if it does not apply.

Adored	Enlightened	Joyful	Strong
Afraid	Enlivened	Lonely	Surprised
Angry	Enraged	Loved	Suspicious
Annoyed	Envious	Loving	Survivor
Anxious	Excited	Mad	Terrified
Apologetic	Exhausted	Nervous	Thrilled
Ashamed	Foolish	Obsessed	Tired
Blessed	Fragile	Pleased	Ugly
Blissful	Frightened	Proud	Unsure
Bothered	Frustrated	Regretful	Upset
Broken	Glad	Relieved	Victim
Cautious	Guilty	Respected	Vulnerable
Confident	Happy	Restless	Worried
Content	Hopeful	Sad	Worthless
Depressed	Hopeless	Satisfied	Worthy
Determined	Horrified	Scared	_____
Disappointed	Hurt	Scattered	_____
Disgusted	Hysterical	Secure	_____
Disturbed	Indifferent	Shy	_____
Embarrassed	Irritated	Smart	_____
Empty	Jealous	Sorry	_____

What **negative** words would you associate with the event that you experienced? (Don't feel as though you have to fill each spot.)

1. _____
2. _____
3. _____
4. _____
5. _____
6. _____
7. _____
8. _____
9. _____
10. _____
11. _____
12. _____

Referring back to the **negative** words that you wrote on the previous page, write down an antonym for each of those words. Some words may not have an antonym, and that is fine. What **positive** word would you use to replace it? (Make sure that these words are written in the same spot as their antonym.)

1. _____
2. _____
3. _____
4. _____
5. _____
6. _____
7. _____
8. _____
9. _____
10. _____
11. _____
12. _____

DAILY AFFIRMATIONS

Rewrite Your Inner Dialog!

Affirmations are words used to declare power and provide emotional encouragement and support! Use the list of words that you just wrote on the previous page as your daily affirmations. Do whatever you have to do to ensure that you speak these words to yourself **daily**! Write the words down on a sticky note and put them all around your home, write them down on your mirror, set a daily alarm on your phone that pops up different affirmations throughout the day. "I am Joyful, because…!" "I am Stronger than I think!" "I am Loved by…!" "I am Worthy of …!" "I am a Survivor!" Do this for thirty days, and I guarantee you will begin to see the change taking place within you!

2 Corinthians 4:13 (NKJV) says, "I believed and therefore I spoke!" I know that can be hard to believe at this moment in your healing journey, but the more you begin to speak these affirmations, the more you will start to believe them. Before you know it, you will be believing and, therefore, speaking all sorts of affirmations and blessings into your life!

Use the calendar below to write down at least one affirmation a day that you can speak to yourself for that particular day. I want you to not just speak that word to yourself, but I also want you to apply it throughout your day. If your word is joyful, then I want you to declare that nothing that happens is going to steal your joy! If your word is strong, then I want you to remind yourself of that word when you are faced with an obstacle that is trying to tell you otherwise!

MONTH-AT-A-GLANCE BLANK CALENDAR

MONTH _____

Sunday	Monday	Tuesday	Wednesday	Thursday	Friday	Saturday

*Use this calendar to track your progress!

IDENTIFYING YOUR TRIGGERS

When using to the term "triggers," I am referring to the person/people, sights, sounds, smells, tastes, physical and emotional feelings that remind you of the trauma you experienced. As we continue to explore your trauma, it is important to identify and combat these triggers so that you are able to regain a sense of your normality.

What **sights** trigger you?

1. _____
2. _____
3. _____
4. _____
5. _____
6. _____
7. _____
8. _____
9. _____
10. _____

What **sounds** trigger you?

1. _____
2. _____
3. _____
4. _____
5. _____
6. _____
7. _____
8. _____
9. _____
10. _____

What **smells** trigger you?

1. _____
2. _____
3. _____
4. _____
5. _____
6. _____
7. _____
8. _____
9. _____
10. _____

What **tastes** trigger you?

1. _____
2. _____
3. _____
4. _____
5. _____
6. _____
7. _____
8. _____
9. _____
10. _____

What **thoughts** trigger you?

1. _____
2. _____
3. _____
4. _____
5. _____
6. _____
7. _____
8. _____
9. _____
10. _____

What type of **surroundings/events** trigger you?

1. _____
2. _____
3. _____
4. _____
5. _____
6. _____
7. _____
8. _____
9. _____
10. _____

What **other things that you can think of** trigger you?

1. _____
2. _____
3. _____
4. _____
5. _____
6. _____
7. _____
8. _____
9. _____
10. _____

STRESSORS

What Is Stress?

Stress is the body's natural reaction to physical, mental, and/or emotional changes (Cleveland Clinic, n.d.). Stress is not always a bad thing. It helps us with self-preservation. Stress is our body's way of making sure that we survive in our everyday environment. If we were walking on a trail and found ourselves face-to-face with a bear, our body's response to that stressor would be to go into fight, flight, or freeze mode. Once we are clear of the danger, our body goes back to its normal state of being. Sometimes, this does not happen. Sometimes, our body feels stressed even when there is no present danger. This heightened level of stress can create adverse effects on our psyche and our bodies.

Three Types of Stress: Acute, Episodic, and Chronic

There are three types of stress: acute stress, episodic acute stress, and chronic stress. According to the American Psychological Association (n.d.), acute stress is stress that occurs in frequent yet small doses. This type of stress is created by certain demands that can arise in the current or near future. This type of stress, when endured for extended periods of time, can create tension headaches, muscle pains, and stomach aches (American Psychological Association, n.d.). Let's say that you are running a few minutes behind in the morning, and now you don't have time to stop for your favorite coffee. Now, you have to suffer through the day with coffee made at the office, which is also known as "mud." This may create some stress, but not anything that is beyond recovery.

Episodic stress occurs when an individual with acute stress has a lot of chaos and crisis in their lives (American Psychological Association, n.d.). Individuals who suffer from episodic acute stress always appear to be in a rush and exude a lot of nervous energy (American Psychological Association, n.d.). Complications that can arise from long-term episodic acute stress are similar to those of acute stress but are more persistent (American Psychological Association, n.d.). These can typically be resolved by making lifestyle changes, creating structure (American Psychological Association, n.d.). Using the same scenario as before, let's say that you are typically fifteen minutes late wherever you go. This will create unnecessary levels of stress. If you begin to make some changes to your nightly or morning routine, it will allow you the additional fifteen minutes needed to get to your destinations on time. This will reduce that stress that is being created by tardiness.

Chronic stress is the type of stress that is responsible for suicidal ideations, heart attacks, strokes, and mental breakdowns (American Psychological Association, n.d.). This type of stress stems from experiencing or witnessing some sort of trauma (American Psychological Association, n.d.). The emotions that were experienced during the event is what makes chronic stress occur (American Psychological Association, n.d.). According to Breedlove and Watson (2018), emotions are subjective and affect an individual's mental state. This is why this type of stress can be associated with the diagnosis of PTSD (American Psychological Association, n.d.). Individuals with PTSD are still experiencing the emotions associated with their trauma.

Now let's say that you were heading back into work for the first time since a fairly serious car accident. You are running a few minutes late, so now you are rushing in order to make up for lost time. On the way into work, you almost get T-boned by a car that ran through a stop sign. This may create a level of stress that causes you to have trouble concentrating and getting through your day.

HOW TO COMBAT STRESS

Developing Your Coping Skills Toolbox

There are several different ways in which someone can lower their stress levels. In this section, we will go over a few different coping skills that can be used when dealing with your triggers and stressors. All of these exercises can be completed in about five to ten minutes.

Deep Breathing

This is an exercise that requires you to really focus on your breathing. I recommend doing this technique in an area where you can sit comfortably and is fairly quiet. Deep breathing allows you to remove stress with the use of cleansing breaths, very similar to yoga, but without the movements. You can enhance your deep breathing techniques by diffusing a therapeutic-grade essential oil and playing soothing music softly in the background.

To begin, sit in a position that is comfortable to you. It can be on the floor or in a chair. Make sure that you are sitting up as straight and as tall as you can comfortably maintain. If you are seated in a chair, make sure that your feet are flat on the floor and are aligned with your hips. Next, you want to close your eyes and place your hand over your chest. For the next several breaths, focus on breathing through your chest. You want to make sure that you breathe slowly in through your nose and out through your mouth. After several breaths, remove your hand from your chest to your abdomen. Repeating the same steps as before, breathe in through your stomach. Again, remember to breathe in through your nose and out through your mouth for several breaths.

Now, you are aware of what it feels like to breathe in through your chest and your abdomen. I want you to begin alternating breathing in through your chest and your abdomen for the next several breaths. Inhale deeply and slowly through your nose, hold it for about three seconds, and then exhale slowly through your mouth.

Progressive Muscle Relaxation Sequence

This is a technique that can be used in conjunction with deep breathing. In order to do this technique, you want to make sure that you are in a comfortable position. Ideally, you want to be in a seated position as this technique can make you sleepy.

Progressive muscle relaxation sequence is just that, relaxing the muscles in a specific sequence. This technique uses the major muscle groups and typically goes from the bottom of the body on up.

You are going to slowly tense the muscles as tightly as you can, holding it for a count of ten seconds, and then you are going relax. As you relax the area, focus on being in the moment and feel the tensions that are of the body leaving. You are going to repeat this on the opposite side and in the same area of the body. So for example, if you are at the beginning of this technique, you are going to focus on the toes on the right side and then switch over to the toes on the left side. You are going to do this same pattern until you have worked your way through the exercise. Make sure that if you are curling toes and releasing twice on the right side, you are doing the same for the left side. You want every area to be equally relaxed. There are areas such as the buttocks, stomach, chest, back, neck, and face in which you do not have to worry about alternating sides.

- Curl your toes downward. Release.
- Point your toes downward using your ankle. Release.
- Tighten your calf muscle by pulling toes toward you using your ankle. Release.
- Squeeze your thigh muscles. Release.
- Squeeze your buttocks. Release.
- Suck your stomach in as far as you can. Release.
- For your chest, breathe in as deep as you can. Release.
- Interlock your hands and squeeze. Release.
- Squeeze your hand into a fist. Release.
- Make a muscle by tightening your biceps, drawing your forearm up and clenching your fist. Release.
- Squeeze your shoulder blades together and arch your back. Release.
- Raise your shoulders up to your ears. Release.
- Open your mouth wide, as though you were yawning. Release.
- Tightly close your eyelids. Release.
- Make a big hard smile as though you are laughing. Release.
- Raise your eyebrows. Release.

Mindfulness

Mindfulness is a skill that allows you to focus on what is occurring in the present moment. When practicing mindfulness, you want to find a place that feels calm and peaceful. Sitting in a position that is most comfortable to you, you are going to close your eyes and focus on your breath.

Feel your breath as it comes and goes; focus on the rise and fall of your chest and belly as you breathe. Notice your body; notice how your feet, legs, arms, hands, shoulders, back, and neck feel.

If you notice your mind beginning to wander, that is okay. Just bring your focus back in on your breath. Do not criticize yourself for your mind's wandering; it is normal. As you begin to practice mindfulness, you will notice that you are able to remain in the moment.

Other Coping Techniques

There are a number of different techniques that can be used to help you cope with triggers. In this section, I want you to be able look into other possible coping techniques that you may enjoy.

_____Writing/Journaling	_____Drawing	_____Coloring
_____Yoga	_____Cardio	_____Boxing
_____Swimming	_____Scrapbooking	_____HIIT
_____Meditation	_____Tai Chi	_____Karate

_____Other:_____

_____Other:_____

_____Other:_____

_____Other:_____

_____Other:_____

_____Other:_____

_____Other:_____

I find these techniques to work best:

_____

_____

_____

_____

_____

_____

_____

_____

_____

_____

THE ROAD TRIP TO RECOVERY

Putting It All Together

What Now?

Now that you have gone through this workbook, what do you do with the information? The first thing for you to do is to take the information that you have worked through and go for a **RIDE!**

How to RIDE through Your Triggers

When your environment triggers negative memories and emotions related a traumatic event that you have experienced, it can be difficult to cope with those emotions. This is where it is going to be imperative that you learn to **RIDE!**

> **Relax.** Referring to one of the coping skills mentioned in this workbook, or another one that you find to be a good fit for you, try to relax yourself.

> **Identify.** After you have begun to relax, try to identify what your trigger was.

> **Decide.** Once the trigger has been identified and you have calmed down, decide on how you are going to respond to the trigger.

> **Execute.** After you have decided on a response, put it into action!

What Does Your RIDE Look Like?

Use the next section to keep track of your triggers, what relaxation technique you found to be useful in calming yourself down during that trigger, and the executed decision that was made. Keeping track of this information will allow you to choose the relaxation techniques that work best during times you are faced with a particular trigger. It will also allow you to figure out which decision is the best to execute in order to overcome the thing that triggered you.

Date:_____   Time:_____

How are you going to **Relax?**

_____

Did it work? (check one) _____yes   _____no

If no, what did you try next?

_____

_____

Identify your trigger?

_____

_____

How are you going to **Decide** to deal with this trigger?

_____

_____

_____

What happened after you **Executed** your decision?

_____

_____

_____

Was this **RIDE** successful? Why or why not?

_____

_____

_____

What would you change?

_____

_____

Date:_____   Time:_____

How are you going to **Relax?**

_____

Did it work? (check one) _____yes   _____no

If no, what did you try next?

_____

_____

Identify your trigger?

_____

_____

How are you going to **Decide** to deal with this trigger?

_____

_____

_____

What happened after you **Executed** your decision?

_____

_____

_____

Was this **RIDE** successful? Why or why not?

_____

_____

_____

What would you change?

_____

_____

Date:_____   Time:_____

How are you going to **Relax?**

_____

Did it work? (check one) _____yes   _____no

If no, what did you try next?

_____

_____

Identify your trigger?

_____

_____

How are you going to **Decide** to deal with this trigger?

_____

_____

_____

What happened after you **Executed** your decision?

_____

_____

_____

Was this **RIDE** successful? Why or why not?

_____

_____

_____

What would you change?

_____

_____

Date:_____   Time:_____

How are you going to **Relax?**

_____

Did it work? (check one) _____yes   _____no

If no, what did you try next?

_____

_____

Identify your trigger?

_____

_____

How are you going to **Decide** to deal with this trigger?

_____

_____

_____

What happened after you **Executed** your decision?

_____

_____

_____

Was this **RIDE** successful? Why or why not?

_____

_____

_____

What would you change?

_____

_____

Date:_____   Time:_____

How are you going to **Relax?**

_____

Did it work? (check one) _____yes   _____no
If no, what did you try next?

_____

_____

Identify your trigger?

_____

_____

How are you going to **Decide** to deal with this trigger?

_____

_____

_____

What happened after you **Executed** your decision?

_____

_____

_____

Was this **RIDE** successful? Why or why not?

_____

_____

_____

What would you change?

_____

_____

FORGIVENESS

What It Is, What It's Not, What It Does, and Why It's Important

It takes a strong person to say they're sorry and an even stronger person to forgive.

—Yolanda Hadid

To forgive is to remove feelings of anger and resentment toward an individual for a mistreatment, wrongdoing, or mistake they made toward you or someone you love. Forgiveness does not mean that you are giving the person/people who you hold responsible for your trauma an excuse for their actions. Forgiveness does not mean that you just forget about what happened to you (and maybe others if you were not the only one) traumatized by the event.

Forgiving the person or people whom you hold responsible for your trauma is not for the person or people. The process of forgiveness is for you! Forgiveness allows you to let go of the hate and bitterness that has built up in your heart. By holding on to the traumatic event, you continue to victimize yourself time after time. This means that you are constantly having to relive what has occurred, giving continued power to the trauma and those who caused it. Here, you are living your life in fear, guilt, shame, and pain, and the offender(s) have moved past the event.

This next section is to be completed once you have truly made up in your mind and in your heart to forgive that person or people whom you hold responsible for your trauma.

Constructing a Letter of Forgiveness to the Person Whom You Hold Responsible for Your Trauma

This Letter of Forgiveness is written to (offender's name/description)

_____

Fill out the sections that apply:

I felt angry…

_____

_____

I felt hurt…

_____

_____

I felt sad/depressed…

_____

_____

I felt betrayed…

_____

_____

I felt broken…

_____

_____

I felt worthless…

_____

_____

I felt ashamed…

_____

_____

I felt stupid…

_____

_____

I felt disgusting…

_____

_____

I felt weak…

_____

_____

You made me feel…

_____
_____
_____
_____
_____
_____

What is something that you have wanted to tell this person or these people about how their actions have affected you?

_____
_____
_____
_____
_____
_____
_____
_____
_____
_____

Are there any other thoughts that you would want to share with them?

_____
_____
_____
_____
_____
_____
_____
_____
_____

Here is where you tell them that you forgive them for the trauma that you hold them responsible for. Make this section as descriptive as you can. If you were to give them the final draft of this letter, you want to make sure that they can recall the very moment of your life that they impacted.

_____
_____
_____
_____
_____

_____

_____

_____

Is this a letter that you would give to the offender(s) if you had the opportunity?
_____Yes   _____No   _____Maybe

How would you feel if given the opportunity to deliver this letter?

_____

_____

_____

_____

TAKING BACK MY IDENTITY

For this next part, I want you to stand in front of a mirror and read this out loud. Pretend that you are reading it to the individual(s) who you feel is responsible for the traumatic event. Read this boldly and with confidence! The more you speak these words to yourself, the more you will begin to believe them and put them into action!

> My experiences that were formed from your choices left me looking at a lesser version of myself. I was unrecognizable to myself. When looking in a mirror I would have to ask, "who is that looking back at me?" I allowed your actions to hold me hostage for far too long, and I am here to tell you that today is the day that I am breaking free. Your words will no longer have power over me! Your actions will no longer dictate my life! I am stronger than you thought I was! The inner critic that you created has been silenced! My inner critic is saying that I am strong, I am brave, and that I am a survivor, not a victim! God said that I am fearfully and wonderfully made, and I am choosing right now in this moment to believe His words! In this moment I am choosing to grow through the traumatic event that you caused. The late 2Pac Shakur wrote about a rose that grew from concrete. He spoke about how people don't look at the scars on its petals, but yet look in amazement at the fact that something so beautiful was able to grow from such a cold, hard place. I am that rose! Your cold and callus act(s) did not retract the beauty that I have! Today I am able to say that **I AM TAKING BACK MY IDENTITY! (Jendayi A. Stafford)**

Now that you have spoken life and words of declaration over yourself, it is time to forgive one more person: **YOURSELF!**

A Letter of Forgiveness to Myself

Dear (your name here) _____,

    I forgive you for…

_____

_____

_____

_____

_____

_____

_____

_____

_____

_____

_____

_____

_____

_____

_____

_____

_____

_____

_____

_____

_____

_____

_____

_____

_____

_____

_____

_____

_____

_____

_____

_____

_____
_____
_____
_____
_____
_____
_____
_____
_____
_____
_____
_____
_____
_____
_____
_____
_____
_____
_____
_____
_____
_____
_____
_____
_____
_____
_____
_____
_____
_____

With love,_____

Signature
Date

WHAT'S NEXT

<<insert image>>

Now that you have completed this workbook, you have had a chance to process one of the most difficult times of your life. You have developed a better understanding of your triggers, identified stressors, and have been given tools to help you combat both those triggers and stressors. Even more, you have forgiven the perpetrator(s) as well as yourself!

<<insert image>>

Reflecting back through all of the work that you have done throughout the workbook, how did you grow through the pain of your experienced trauma?

_____
_____
_____
_____
_____
_____
_____

Did you find a purpose in the pain that you have experienced?
_____Yes   _____No_____I'm still not sure

What was/is the purpose for the pain?

_____
_____
_____
_____
_____
_____
_____

What are you planning on doing with the new understanding of that purpose?

_____
_____
_____
_____
_____
_____
_____

What are some of the biggest takeaways from this journey that I have just been on?

_____
_____
_____
_____
_____
_____
_____
_____

_____
_____
_____
_____
_____
_____
_____
_____
_____
_____

Using the following self-assessment, please rate your progress from when you first started this workbook until now.

1. I have more confidence in myself:

    Strongly Disagree   **Disagree**   **Neutral**   **Agree**   **Strongly Agree**

2. My trauma no longer holds power over me:

    Strongly Disagree   **Disagree**   **Neutral**   Agree   **Strongly Agree**

3. I can identify my stressors:

    Strongly Disagree   **Disagree**   **Neutral**   **Agree**   **Strongly Agree**

4. I can identify my triggers:

    Strongly Disagree   **Disagree**   **Neutral**   **Agree**   **Strongly Agree**

5. I feel as though I have the tools needed to combat both my stressors and triggers:

    Strongly Disagree   **Disagree**   **Neutral**   Agree   **Strongly Agree**

6. I feel less angry about the trauma:

    Strongly Disagree   **Disagree**   **Neutral**   **Agree**   **Strongly Agree**

7. I feel less broken and hurt by the trauma:

    Strongly Disagree   **Disagree**   **Neutral**   **Agree**   **Strongly Agree**

8. I feel as though I have found my self-worth:

    Strongly Disagree   **Disagree**   **Neutral**   **Agree**   **Strongly Agree**

9. I have found a purpose to the pain:

    Strongly Disagree   **Disagree**   **Neutral**   **Agree**   **Strongly Agree**

10. I plan on using this workbook to work through another traumatic event:

    Strongly Disagree   **Disagree**   **Neutral**   **Agree**   **Strongly Agree**

Scoring: for questions 1–10, assign the appropriate numerical value to your response and add the numbers for your total score.

Strongly Disagree: one point
Disagree: two points
Neutral: three points
Agree: four points
Strongly Agree: five points

1. _____   2. _____   3. _____   4. _____   5. _____
6. _____   7. _____   8. _____   9. _____   10. _____

Total Score: _____

If your score is between:

Ten to thirty points—I strongly suggest that you seek professional counseling to help you continue on through your journey of overcoming your trauma. You should be proud of the progress that you have made no matter how minute. You still have some things to work through, and you may not be able to deal with it all by yourself. Contact a local therapist so that you can continue your triumph over your trauma in a safe, therapeutic environment.

Thirty-one to fifty points—I suggest that you continue to make forward progression in your journey of triumph over your trauma. You should be proud of the progress that you have made thus far. Continue making forward progression.

Remember…

Regardless of your score, if you feel as though you need to talk to someone, please refer back to the resources that were provided in the beginning of the book. Also, reach out to a local therapist. Try to find one that is specifically trained in or has experience in working with trauma patients. If you cannot find a therapist that specializes in trauma, remember, all licensed therapists are trained to help you navigate through a variety of mental and emotional challenges. Remember, every therapist is different; and therefore, their therapeutic styles vary. Don't give up on the first therapist that you see. Stick it out! Your discomfort may be causing you to want to run away from the therapy. With that being said, if there are definite red flags or you don't feel as though you are connecting well with your therapist, try asking them to refer you to another therapists. Remember, the therapeutic process should be a collaborative process.

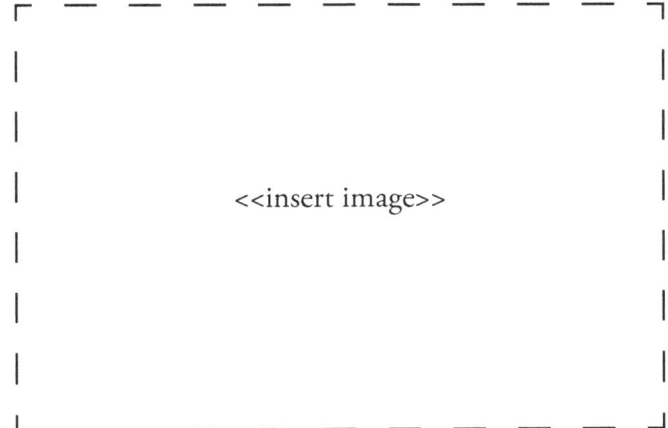

<<insert image>>

You did it! You made it to the end of this workbook. Regardless of your progress, you should be so proud of yourself. You made a conscious choice to take the steps necessary to triumph over the trauma that tried to break you!

I am proud of you! I know that I do not personally know you, but I know the strength and courage that it takes to acknowledge when we are not mentally doing well. It took courage to realize and acknowledge that your past trauma was still holding power over you. It took courage to purchase this workbook. It took even more strength and courage to complete this workbook! Despite your progress, you are a stronger and more courageous person for putting in the work required to TRIUMPH over the trauma! Continue making forward progress. Your journey is not over because you have completed this workbook. This is a conscious lifelong process. There is always going to be something that tries to derail your progress; but with your new tools, you can now be better prepared.

—Jendayi A. Stafford

NOTES

NOTES

ABOUT THE AUTHOR

Jendayi A. Stafford is a therapist, a child mental health specialist (CMHS), a certified child and adolescent trauma professional (CATP), a public speaker, as well as a published author and co-author. She earned a masters in psychology with an emphasis in marriage and family therapy, a masters in organizational leadership, and a graduate certificate in human resource management from Brandman University. She is currently working toward her PhD in developmental psychology at Walden University.

Jendayi is the founder and owner of Mission Counseling & Consulting, LLC. Mission Counseling & Consulting, LLC provides a number of services including whole-body holistic health coaching, aptitude enrichment consulting, business and program development and an online academy; I.N.K. Academy. Through her company and online academy, Jendayi hosts a number of various workshops, seminars and trainings spanning across many different subjects including self-esteem, emotion regulation, trauma, writing and publishing, and personal development.